BIBLE STORIES

AN AWESOME ADVENTURE

Jesus Is Calling

Edited by Ken Ham

Original text: Albert Hari, Charles Singer
English text: Anne White, Noel Kelly

Illustrations: Mariano Valsesia, Betti Ferrero

The First Friends

Fra Angelico (1400 - 1455)

Decorated letter from the missal
The Call of St. Peter and St. Andrew

© Orsi Battaglini-Giraudon / Museo di San Marco, Florence, Italy

At the Lake

View over Nazareth.

For about 30 years Jesus lived in Nazareth. One day He left His family, His friends, and His village. He knew that He was sent by God to preach the gospel far beyond His own little village.

About 30 kilometers (18 miles) east of Nazareth are the clear waters of Lake Tiberias,* teeming with fish. Jesus saw the fishermen busy with their boats and their nets. Jesus spoke with them.

He called the fishermen to follow Him and to share His work. The four He called were brothers from two different families: Simon and his brother Andrew and James and his brother John.

* Lake Tiberias *is also called the Lake of Gennesaret or the Sea of Galilee. It lies between the green hills of Galilee and the desert peaks of Syria, and is 21 kms (13 mi.) long and 12 kms (7-1/2 mi.) wide.*

Lake Tiberias.

About Forty Years Later

Mark wrote his Gospel account within just a few years after Jesus' death, resurrection, and ascension, probably in Rome. At this time Simon (whom Jesus named Peter) and James had probably been put to death for following Jesus. Mark may not have been present at the lakeside, but it is thought that Peter himself may have told him how his first meeting with Jesus transformed his life. Peter had been a simple fisherman until Jesus invited him to become a "fisher" of men and women.

A fisherman from Sri Lanka.

3

Come and Follow Me!

From the Gospel according to Mark (1:14-20)

Now after that John was put in prison, Jesus came into Galilee, preaching the gospel of the kingdom of God, And saying, The time is fulfilled, and the kingdom of God is at hand: repent ye, and believe the gospel.

Now as he walked by the sea of Galilee, he saw Simon and Andrew his brother casting a net into the sea: for they were fishers. And Jesus said unto them, Come ye after me, and I will make you to become fishers of men. And straightway they forsook their nets, and followed him.

And when he had gone a little further thence, he saw James the son of Zebedee, and John his brother, who also were in the ship mending their nets. And straightway he called them: and they left their father Zebedee in the ship with the hired servants, and went after him.

Kingdom of God

In Jesus' day this phrase made people think of a time when everyone would be happy, living according to God's Word. The kingdom (or reign) of God is like a seed that has been planted, and like yeast put into a batch of dough. It has already begun, yet it is still to grow and come into its fullness. This is happening just as God promised to Abraham way back in Genesis 22:18.

The Good News

In Greek the word gospel (*euaggelion*) means "good news." It is the announcement that God is coming to take away His peoples' sins and make them happy forever through His Son, the Lord Jesus Christ, as they receive the forgiveness of their sins by God's grace through faith in Jesus' name. Jesus

announced the good news to the poor. His apostles are sent to bring this message to the whole world.

Zebedee

In Hebrew, Zebedee means "gift from God." In English we would say "God-given."

His Call

The Day May Come

The day may come when you will have to leave your family, the close circle where you feel at home and loved. There may be a day when you have to leave familiar people, places, and things in order to follow God's call in your life (Matthew 19:29; Luke 9:57-62).

The Mission of Jesus

The day came when Jesus knew that He must leave His family and His village, to begin the mission which His Father (God) had entrusted to Him: to proclaim God's love and salvation to the world.

Call

When you need someone to undertake a special job, to carry out a mission, you "call" him or her by name. "Come on . . . ! We need you and your skills to share in this great mission." Jesus is calling His disciples today, just as He did when He walked the earth.

Response

Anyone who is called to a special task feels challenged. They wonder: Can I do this? Is it really me you want? Some may think the same thoughts when Jesus calls them to follow Him. But disciples of Jesus are to take comfort in God's Word when He says, "I will never leave thee, nor forsake thee" (Hebrews 13:5). God is able to perform through us whatever it may be that He calls us to do for His sake (2 Timothy 1:12).

Together

The work to which Jesus calls people is challenging. It can seem daunting, but you are not called on your own. Remember, Jesus promises to be with His people always, and you will have other Christians who will be serving God with you also. With God, all things are possible. Through faith, mountains can be moved!

Those Who Say Yes

They are all ages,
women, men, and children.
They are from near and far:
workers, artists, students, the
unemployed, rich and poor,
powerful and ordinary.
They come from all corners of the
world to work together for God and
His kingdom.

The call of Jesus has reached them,
touching their hearts and minds,
changing their lives.
They have been called to follow Jesus,
to believe in Him and to entrust
themselves completely to Him.

They have been called and chosen
to follow Jesus Christ, such as they
are, big or small, brave or weak —
sinners saved by grace through
faith in Him, and to go with
Him, no matter how difficult
the road may be, to
accomplish the mission that
Jesus entrusts to them:
to announce the love and
salvation of God to
the ends of
the earth!

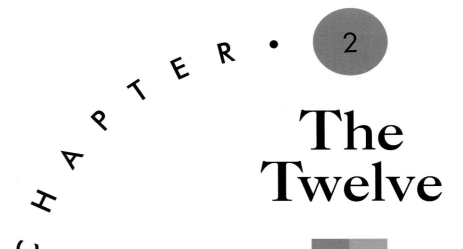

CHAPTER · 2

The
Twelve

Fra Angelico (1400-1455)

Sermon on the Mount
(after restoration)

© Orsi Battaglini - Giraudon / Museo di San Marco, Florence, Italy

They Followed Jesus

Sculpture of St. Peter in the Church of St. Peter in Chains.

Jesus did not work alone. He called a group of 12, a number recalling the 12 tribes of Israel. These 12 were called to stay with Jesus and then to be sent out. The leader of the group was Peter. Judas was in charge of the money. The Twelve stayed with Jesus until His arrest. Jesus was betrayed by Judas. When Jesus was arrested, all the others ran away.

The Work Continued

The Twelve were not the only ones Jesus called. There was also a larger group of 70 disciples which is often forgotten (see Luke 10).*

After His death, resurrection, and ascension, when on the Day of Pentecost the Holy Spirit was poured out upon them, the disciples regained their courage. They came to understand in a new way what the presence ("being with Him") and mission ("being sent by Him") meant. They were to carry the good news of salvation to the ends of the earth (Acts 1).

The example of new apostles like Paul encouraged them to be even bolder in proclaiming the good news. The women played an important role in welcoming groups of Christians to their homes. When the Christian communities retold the story of the call of the Twelve, they could see that they too were continuing the mission for which the Twelve had been prepared.

The Story

Sculpture of Mary Magdalene in Lestelle-Batharam in France.

* Jesus included a group of women to be among His followers. Among the women who followed Jesus and are spoken of in the gospel, we can mention "Mary called Magdalene, out of whom went seven devils, and Joanna the wife of Chuza Herod's steward, and Susanna, and many others" (Luke 8:2-3). Jesus' mother Mary, and His mother's sister(John 19:25), "and Mary, the mother of James and Joses, and the mother of Zebedee's children" (Matthew 27:56).

9

Jesus Calls the Twelve

From the Gospel according to Mark (3:13-19)

And he goeth up into a mountain, and calleth unto him whom he would: and they came unto him. And he ordained twelve, that they should be with him, and that he might send them forth to preach, And to have power to heal sicknesses, and to cast out devils: And Simon he surnamed Peter; And James the son of Zebedee, and John the brother of James; and he surnamed them Boanerges, which is, The sons of thunder: And Andrew, and Philip, and Bartholomew, and Matthew, and Thomas, and James the son of Alphaeus, and Thaddaeus, and Simon the Canaanite, And Judas Iscariot, which also betrayed him: and they went into an house.

What Do the Names of the 12 Apostles Mean?

Peter: rock or stone
John: God is gracious
James: (Jacob, "supplanter")
*   he will take the place of*
Andrew: manly
Philip: lover of horses
Bartholomew: son of Tolmai
Matthew: gift of God
Thomas: twin
James, son of Alphaeus: son
*   of the leader (or chief)*
Jude: praise
Simon the Canaanite (also
*   Simon the Zealot)*
*   freedom-fighter*
Judas Iscariot: the man from
*   Kerioth, land of ravines*
*   (near Hebron)*

Why Twelve?

Twelve is not just a random number. It has a deeper meaning. It signifies completeness. There were 12 tribes in Israel. There are 12 months in the year. Jesus chose 12 apostles. Perhaps the idea is that of "divine government."

Mission

Team

It is impossible to succeed in any big project without gathering a chosen team. The team members God chooses are called the "Church." The Church puts into practice the plan God himself has made. The true Church dedicates itself completely to the task God has ordained for it.

Variety

The strength of a team and its ability to be creative stem from its different members. Different ideas are needed, different characters, different minds, backgrounds, and ways of going about things. So the skills of each person will help the task to be completed.

Unique

Each person has his or her own special place on the team. Their talents and know-how make them unique because they are God-given. In a team each one plays the essential part which is his or hers alone.

Mission

The team gathered together by Jesus is made up of all those who answer His call, obey His commandments, and who put God's Word into practice. To that team — the Church — Jesus entrusts the mission of proclaiming the good news of God's love and salvation.

Apostles and Disciples

Each person Christ saves from his or her sins is called to be a witness and an ambassador for Him. Each Christian, filled with the Holy Spirit and the gifts of body and spirit, is appointed by Jesus to be His emissary, His envoy, His messenger sent to make God's love and salvation visible to the world.

The followers of Jesus (other than the Twelve) are also known as "disciples" (those who learn).

Still Counting!

How numerous are
the disciples of Christ!
All over the world they
are answering His call.
What do they do today?
They forgive those who do wrong.
They reveal the power of gentleness.
They love God and their neighbors
as themselves with a love that
overcomes everything.
And they preach the gospel
(good news) of Jesus Christ to
everyone who will listen.

What do they do today?
They hold out healing hands.
They overcome the poison of
jealousy. They break bread together.
They pray to their Father in heaven
and present the offer of salvation
to the world.

Do you want your name
on God's list of
disciples today?

Unwelcome

Paolo Caliari
also known as **Véronèse**
(1528-1588)

The Banquet at
Levi's House

© Giraudon - Collection particulière, Paris, France

It's a Scandal!

Customs officers and tax collectors (often called publicans) were very unpopular in Israel. People accused them of getting rich illegally, of demanding more in taxes than the state required, and of pocketing the difference for themselves.* The Pharisees blamed them for having contact with the pagans, and by doing so they were viewed as being impure. They were treated without respect.

Jesus' behavior was surprising. He called a customs officer, Levi the son of Alphaeus, to follow Him. Levi organized a meal at home with his publican friends, and invited Jesus and His disciples. The scribes of the Pharisee group said it was a scandal, "Why eateth your Master with publicans and sinners?" Jesus explained His action, "I am not come to call the righteous, but sinners to repentance" (Matthew 9:11, 13).

A Real Welcome

A woman making bread in Egypt.

Collection of tea leaves.

After the death, resurrection, and ascension of Jesus, Christians used to come together to eat, to pray, to study the Scriptures, and to remember Jesus. Soon problems arose. The rich took the best places and the poor were left to one side. Some Christians of Jewish origin refused to share the meal with Christians of pagan origin.

The example of Jesus, who ate with publicans and sinners, helped the first Christians to understand that they were called to welcome everybody around the same table. In God's sight, His people, whom He has saved from their sins, are neither Jew nor pagan, slave nor free, male nor female (Galatians 3:28; Colossians 3:11).

Harvesting tea leaves.

The people of Jesus' time were burdened by many taxes. Under the law of the Roman Empire they had to pay land tax, people tax, road tax, and taxes on bridges and markets. The publicans were in charge of collecting this money. Besides this, the Jews paid a Temple tax and tithes (a tenth) on the land and any produce that they grew.

Jesus and Levi

From the Gospel according to Mark (2:13-17)

And he went forth again by the sea side; and all the multitude resorted unto him, and he taught them. And as he passed by, he saw Levi the son of Alphaeus sitting at the receipt of custom, and said unto him, Follow me. And he arose and followed him.

And it came to pass, that, as Jesus sat at meat in his house, many publicans and sinners sat also together with Jesus and his disciples: for there were many, and they followed him. And when the scribes and Pharisees saw him eat with publicans and sinners, they said unto his disciples, How is it that he eateth and drinketh with publicans and sinners?

When Jesus heard it he saith unto them, They that are whole have no need of the physician, but they that are sick: I came not to call the righteous, but sinners to repentance.

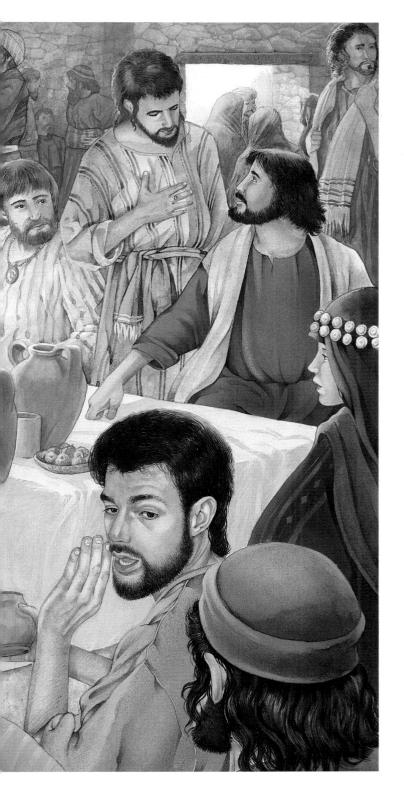

Levi

The "Levi" of whom the Scripture text speaks is probably "Matthew the publican (Matthew 10:3) the author of the Gospel record which bears his name.

"Follow Me!"

In the gospel, to "follow" someone does not just mean to walk behind them. To follow Jesus means to surrender your life to Him, to share His life and deeds, to believe in Him, to turn from sin, to trust Him completely, to be obedient to Him, and to be ready to give your life for Him.

Pharisees

The Pharisees were fanatical about the Jewish law. They wanted to make it apply right down to the smallest detail, in ways that God never intended. The gospel records often showed them as being overbearing, legalistic, and hypocritical.

Change

Goodness

No human being, except the Lord Jesus Christ, is without sin. Being good means trying to follow the example of Jesus: loving God above all else, and our neighbors as ourselves.

Sinner

Everyone is a sinner because we all give in to evil sometimes and do wrong. But God's people do not remain trapped forever in their sins. Being a sinner means turning away from God's commandments and the example of Jesus, and living far from the love of God and neighbor. It means falling short of God's perfect character and His laws.

Labels

It is easy to label some people by calling them "good" or "evil." But according to God, and not your opinion, we are all evil (not perfect) in God's sight. God says, "There is none righteous, no not one" (Romans 3:10).

Change

Just because someone sins does not mean that they are beyond the salvation that Christ brings! Everyone who believes the gospel, having been saved by God's grace through faith in Jesus' atonement, through the regenerating work of the Holy Spirit, will be changed. They will become new creations in Jesus Christ. After that, when evil appears, God's people can then be empowered to resist it.

Not Rejected but Loved

Jesus will not reject anyone who comes to Him in faith (John 6:37). Those who come by faith and repentance, seeking God's forgiveness through Christ, will be saved from eternal condemnation. He calls His people to turn from their sins and respond to His love and offer of salvation. In God's sight, all those who receive the gift of salvation are His children.

All
Alike

Alike:
We are all the same.
We all have sinned and come
short of God's glory, perfection,
and holiness.

One day we are full of generosity
giving without counting, and the
next day fired up with temper
and full of anger!

One day my lips bear
the sun's own smile,
and then on another day
my mouth spits out mocking words
which slice deeper than a knife.

All alike
we are sinners!
God says that the hearts of people
need to be changed
And that they need to be
born again
from above.
God calls His people
to trust in Him
And He gives His people
the chance to live in the
light of Christ,
in His image
and likeness!

CHAPTER 4

The Rich Young Man

Painted mural of Christ
in the monastery of
Eski Gumus, Turkey

© F. Zvardon

A Newcomer

Young Palestinian on a donkey.

Lots of people were following Jesus. Some had left everything to be with him. Peter, Andrew, and John left their fishing business; Levi abandoned his work at the tax desk. Others traveled great distances from their homes, families, and villages. Some were poor, with neither possessions, jobs, nor families.

One day a young man came and said to Him, "Good Master, what good thing shall I do, that I may have eternal life? And he said unto him, Why callest thou me good? There is none good but one, that is God: but if thou wilt enter into life, keep the commandments. He saith unto him, Which? Jesus said, Thou shalt do no murder, Thou shalt not commit adultery, Thou shalt not steal, Thou shalt not bear false witness, Honour thy father and thy mother: and, Thou shalt love thy neighbour as thyself. The young man saith unto him, All these things have I kept from my youth up: what lack I yet? Jesus said unto him, If thou wilt be perfect, go and sell that thou hast, and give to the poor, and thou shalt have treasure in heaven: and come and follow me. But when the young man heard that saying, he went away sorrowful: for he had great possessions" (Matthew 19:16-22).*

Need for Repentance and Faith

Mark also told this story to the rich and poor Christians in his community (Mark 10). The point was that Jesus loved them too, just as He loved the man who rushed up to Him. Jesus also exposed the misunderstanding that it is possible for people to keep God's commandments perfectly in order that they may earn their way to Heaven. Remember, we are all sinners, and no one can keep God's laws perfectly. Jesus was showing people that they need to completely rely on His death which was to come on the cross (His atonement) *alone* for the forgiveness of their sins and entrance into eternal life.

T h e   S t o r y

Statue from the garden of the Israel Museum in Jerusalem.

Carrying bricks in Nepal.

* Jesus taught that following Him means sacrificing things that we may love — a person must not love anyone or anything more than God. By making these sacrifices Christians show God and others that they love Him above everything else. Some Christians had already sold their goods and shared the money with the poor. The joy of sharing is worth more than the sadness of everyone looking after himself or herself only.

Bible

Salvation Is from God

From the Gospel according to Mark (10:23-30)

And Jesus looked round about, and saith unto his disciples, How hardly shall they that have riches enter into the kingdom of God!

And the disciples were astonished at his words. But Jesus answereth again, and saith unto them, Children, how hard is it for them that trust in riches to enter into the kingdom of God! It is easier for a camel to go through the eye of a needle, than for a rich man to enter into the kingdom of God.

And they were astonished out of measure, saying among themselves, Who then can be saved?

And Jesus looking upon them saith, With men it is impossible, but not with God: for with God all things are possible.

Then Peter began to say unto him, Lo, we have left all, and have followed thee.

And Jesus answered and said, Verily I say unto you, There is no man that hath left house, or brethren, or sisters, or father, or mother, or wife, or children, or lands, for my sake, and the gospel's, But he shall receive an hundredfold now in this time, houses, and brethren, and sisters, and mothers, and children, and lands, with persecutions; and in the world to come eternal life.

Good Master

Jesus is not a master like the others. Jesus is the Son of God — He is both God and man. He was the only perfect human who ever lived. Even in light of that, Jesus reserved the title of "good" for God the Father alone.

Commandments

The Ten Commandments are part of the law of Moses which God gave to Israel through Moses (see Exodus 20).

He Went Away

The young man's self-righteousness and love of money kept him from seeing his personal need for Jesus. He also failed to see his need to be forgiven by God for all of his sins, thinking that he could earn his way to heaven through keeping God's commandments. The Bible tells us that we can't earn or work our way to heaven by trying to be perfect in God's sight.

Decisions

Riches

To be rich in material ways is not a bad thing in itself. Yet with material wealth comes great responsibility. Being rich in material things can become bad when those riches are loved more than God. Jesus said that we are to store up heavenly treasures (Luke 12:21; Matthew 6:20). Christians do not need to worry about tomorrow because God promised that He would provide for us (Matthew 6:7, 25-26).

Following One True God

Jesus will not reject *anyone* who comes to Him in faith — that includes rich people also. He does, however, warn His people of the danger of ending up prisoners, attached to the wealth they possess and not seeing their need to be saved from the bondage that accompanies their sins if they don't repent. Jesus said, "No man can serve two masters: for either he will hate the one, and love the other; or else he will hold to the one, and despise the other. Ye cannot serve God and mammon [money]" (Matthew 6:24).

To Follow Jesus . . .

How can we truly follow Jesus if we are imprisoned in any way?

. . . Wholeheartedly

It's the road of love that we take with Jesus. On that road people share; they do not just look after themselves. On that road, with Jesus, people do not just give a bit; they give wholeheartedly!

Free to Choose

Jesus allows His people freedom to choose. When Jesus sets His people free from the bondage to their sinful nature, He sets them free to serve God. Only then do they become truly free to serve and worship God in Spirit and truth (John 4:23). When all is said and done, Christ will give eternal rewards and

blessings to all those who have faithfully served Him in this life.

Treasures

What priceless treasures
you possess: God gives each
one of us gifts, the joy of a
smile, the skills of our hands
and our intelligence!
Will you share them generously
for Jesus and with others?

What riches you possess!

What about the words from your lips!
Will you use them to worship God,
to encourage others, and share the
good news of Jesus Christ?

What about the strength of your courage?
Will you use it to lift up those who fall
under the weight of sorrow?

What about the happiness of your life?
Will you use it to surround with light
those who are downtrodden?

What about the joy of the Lord
in your life? Will you share it
And shine your light on those
who are in the dark,
and lost in this world?

What treasures you have
in Jesus Christ!
Will you use them
as you follow Him?

A Demanding Road

Decorated letter "D"
from the missal
Entrance into Jerusalem
circa 1500

© Bridgeman-Giraudon / Wallace Collection, Londres (Angleterre)

Knowing Where You're Going

The Roman Coliseum in Italy.

Some people thought that they were following Jesus for the right reasons. Some people thought He would overthrow the Romans.* They were hoping for a good place in the kingdom that Jesus proclaimed. Jesus did not mislead them. He told them that it would not always be easy and they would have to carry their crosses daily.

What many people didn't realize was that Jesus came to set His people free, not from Roman occupation, but from something far worse — their sins. He came to save His people from a much more horrifying situation — the eternal destruction of their souls in hell!

Jesus prepared to go to Jerusalem where He would face the civic and religious leaders, and die on the cross for the sins of His people. Tragically, the religious leaders there in Jerusalem did not agree with Jesus' message. To go to Jerusalem meant laying down His life. Eventually He would be crucified, which was God's plan.

Remembering the Words of Jesus

There are some words that renew our courage. A long time later, when the early Christians read the words of Jesus in Luke's Gospel account, they had a better understanding of the difficulties they faced because of the Gospel: separation from their families, having to travel to spread the good news, and the problems of daily life.

Bridge in Carpates, Romania.

Statue of a Roman soldier on the Victor Emmanuel Bridge in Rome, Italy.

* At the time of Jesus, the country of Israel was occupied by Roman legions. Pontius Pilate, a representative of the emperor of Rome, controlled all of the country. Many people in Jesus' day were hoping to be set free from this occupation.

Carrying Your Cross

From the Gospel according to Luke (9:57-62; 9:23)

And it came to pass, that, as they went in the way, a certain man said unto him, Lord, I will follow thee whithersoever thou goest.

And Jesus said unto him, Foxes have holes, and birds of the air have nests; but the Son of man hath not where to lay his head.

And he said unto another, Follow me.

But he said, Lord, suffer me first to go and bury my father.

Jesus said unto him, Let the dead bury their dead: but go thou and preach the kingdom of God.

And another also said, Lord, I will follow thee; but let me first go bid them farewell, which are at home at my house.

And Jesus said unto him, No man, having put his hand to the plough, and looking back, is fit for the kingdom of God.

And he said to them all, If any man will come after me, let him deny himself, and take up his cross daily, and follow me.

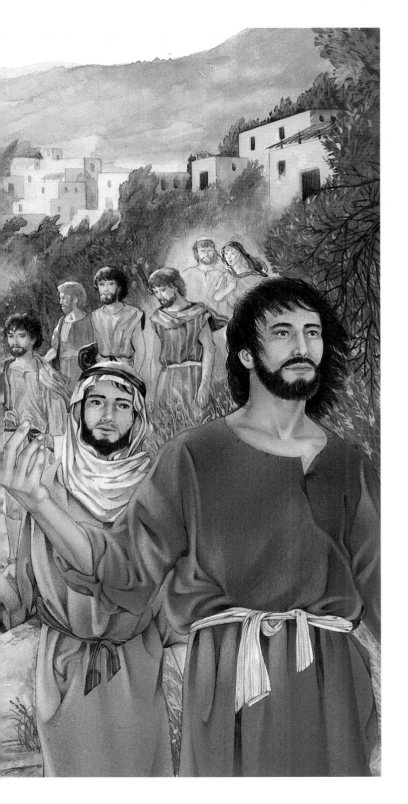

Cross

The cross was an instrument of terrible and humiliating torture. Gradually the followers of Jesus understood that, like Him, they too had to "carry their cross" every day.

Son of Man

This phrase recalls a vision from the prophet Daniel (sometime around the middle of the sixth century B.C.) He describes the coming of the Son of Man on the clouds of heaven to save from judgment those who are His own (Daniel 7:13-14). The first Christians understood that Jesus is the Son of Man, the Messiah, who was to come at the promised time (Matthew 9:6, 12:40).

On the Road

After leaving His village of Nazareth, Jesus traveled all around the country. He was often on the road. When people heard His words and saw what He did, many of them wanted to follow Him.

The Way of Jesus

The Creator God Became a Man

Jesus is not a revolutionary or a philosopher with new ideas. Nor is He a teacher thinking up interesting theories. Jesus is the Creator God who became the Saviour of the world to set His own creation free from *sin, death,* and *the curse (Genesis 3).* Jesus is the Son of God who came to teach His people to live in the love of God and neighbor. He is the "last Adam" who came to undo the works of the devil and to reverse the curse of death that the "first Adam" brought upon all creation (Genesis 1, 2, and 3; 1 Corinthians 15:21-22; Romans 5, 12, and 14; Romans 8:8-30).

A Difficult Road

The road to which Jesus calls His friends is hard. Jesus calls them to forsake their sins, give up being self-centered, to leave pride behind, to stop being small-minded, to carry the burden of others, to believe in Him without seeing Him, and to bear the mocking and humiliation that sometimes comes with being a follower of Him.

A New Road

The road to which Jesus calls us is completely new! It is a road where you pray for your enemies, where you forgive others, where you share sacrificially, where you place yourself completely into the hands of God the Father.

A Road of Love

Jesus calls us to love God above all else, and our neighbors as ourselves! If we do this, then we have fulfilled all of God's laws and commandments (Mark 12:30). Jesus proclaims that only the love of God in our hearts is able to transform the world.

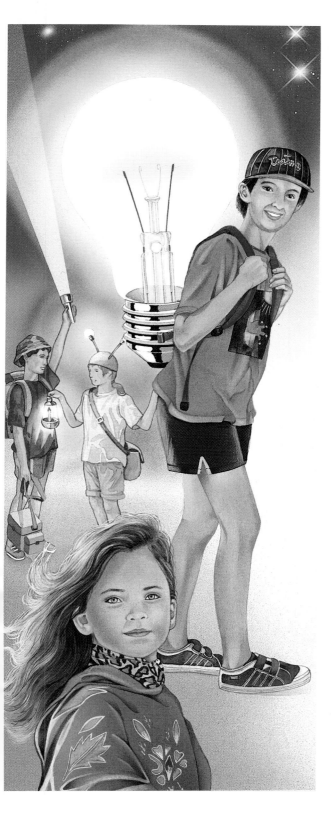

On
the Way

They set out on the road
with the unforgettable
words of Jesus
singing in their hearts
and in their lives.

They set out,
opening their arms
to those who are
wounded by daily
worries and fear.
They set out to offer
the gift of salvation through
faith in Jesus Christ.

The unforgettable
words of Jesus
burn like flames of fire
in their memory.
And these words
are a daily call,
urging them to
continue on earth
proclaiming the gospel
and sharing the
love of God
with everyone
they meet.

Jesus' Country

Characteristics

Israel was a small, poor country. From Nazareth to Jerusalem it is only about 114 kilometers (70 miles). It had been occupied by Roman troops since 63 B.C. Israel is a land with a long history, at the crossroads of civilization and continents.

Ruins of a synagogue in Jerusalem.

The Regions

In the north is Galilee which has a pleasant climate, charming villages, and a clear water lake. In the center is the hilly region of Samaria. The inhabitants of this region, the Samaritans, are shunned by their neighbors. In the south is Judea, a mountainous region, partly desert, with a harsh climate.

The Towns

The Roman authorities had their headquarters in Caesarea, a coastal city, and Jewish authorities had their headquarters in Jerusalem, the capital. It was the religious center of the country because the Temple was there. Jesus was crucified in Jerusalem. Bethlehem, the ancient city of David, is the birthplace of Jesus.

The Jordan River Valley in Judea.

However, He spent the largest part of His life in Nazareth, a little village in Galilee. He began His public ministry in the Capernaum area, the town of the apostle Peter.

Geography

To the west lay the Mediterranean Sea, often called the "Great Sea." To the east the river Jordan flows in a deep valley through Lake Tiberias and south toward the Dead Sea, which in Jesus' day was called the "Salt Sea."

The country can be divided into four strips, each parallel to the sea:

1. A coastal plain narrowing toward the north.
2. A mountain chain where some peaks are over 1,000 meters (3,200 feet) high. It is desert-like in the south, with rich valleys in the north.
3. The deepest trench in the world on land is the Jordan River Valley. The surface of the Dead Sea is about 400 meters (1,300 feet) below sea level.
4. Various plateaus are beyond the Jordan. Certain peaks are more than 1,200 meters (3,900 feet) high.

Today

Lake Tiberias, also known as the Sea of Galilee.

The largest part of the country where Jesus lived now belongs to the state of Israel. The neighboring countries are Lebanon to the north, Syria and Jordan to the east, and Egypt to the south.

THE BAD NEWS

The word "gospel" means "good news" — the good news that Jesus Christ our Creator came to earth to die on a cross and be raised from the dead. However, many people have forgotten why this is good news. First of all, they need to understand the bad news related to us in the Book of Genesis.

In Genesis 3 we first read of this bad news — the account of the origin of sin, when the first man, Adam, rebelled against his Creator. Sadly, there are many people today who believe this account in Genesis to be just an allegory or myth. However, if this is so, then the message of the good news about Jesus Christ would only be an allegory also!

Paul explains to us in 1 Corinthians 15 that Jesus Christ is the "last Adam." In other words, because there was a literal first Adam who because of his actions, brought sin and the penalty of death into the world, then God sent His Son, the Lord Jesus Christ, to be a literal last Adam! The last Adam, through His death, brought life — eternal life in heaven to those who trust in Him.

THE GOOD NEWS

The good news about God's Son and His death and resurrection can only be understood when the account in Genesis is accepted as real history. In fact, the good news about Jesus is first given in Genesis 3:15, "And I will put enmity between thee and the woman, between thy seed and her seed; it shall bruise thy head and thou shalt bruise his heel." This is a prophecy concerning the coming of Christ to save all those who believe in Him from their sin.

Because of sin, we are condemned to eternal separation from God. And the good news? Praise the Lord, He calls us to follow Him so we can have that peace and joy of knowing that when we die, we will be with our Creator forever!

Just as Jesus called disciples to follow Him when He was on earth, so He is calling us today to also be His disciples. And what does it mean to follow Jesus? It means you must surrender your life to Him, to share His life and deeds, to believe in Him, to turn from sin, to trust Him completely, to be obedient to Him, and to be ready to give your life to Him.

Jesus calls His people to turn from their sins and respond to His love and offer of salvation. Those who come by faith and repentance, seeking God's forgiveness through Christ, will be saved from eternal condemnation.

As you read this book that tells of the good news (the gospel) and the call to follow Jesus, think of a relative, friend, or neighbor to whom you can explain this wonderful message of hope — and lead them to be disciples of our Lord and Saviour.

Ken Ham
Executive Director
Answers in Genesis

Answers in Genesis is a non-profit, Christ-centered, evangelistic ministry.

An Awesome Adventure Titles Now Available:

- Jesus the Child
- Jesus Is Calling

Upcoming Titles Available Soon:

- The Creation Story
- Abraham's Family
- Jesus Heals
- Who Is Jesus
- Moses
- The Promised Land

Jesus
Is Calling

Edited by
Ken Ham

TEXT

Albert HARI - Charles SINGER

PHOTOGRAPHY

Frantisek ZVARDON

Alsace MÉDIA

Patrice THÉBAULT

ILLUSTRATIONS

Mariano VALSESIA

Betti FERRERO

MIA. Milan Illustrations Agency

FIRST PRINTING: FEBRUARY 1998

For information write: Master Books, P.O. Box 727, Green Forest, AR 72638.

ISBN: 0-89051-196-9

ÉDITIONS
DU SIGNE

© ÉDITIONS DU SIGNE 1997